P9-ARR-640

Ace Your Math Test

MULTIPLICATION AND DIVISION

Ace your Math Test

Rebecca Wingard-Nelson

Enslow Publishers, Inc.
40 Industrial Road
Box 398
Berkeley Heights, NJ 07922
USA
http://www.enslow.com

Library of Congress Cataloging-in-Publication Data
Wingard-Nelson, Rebecca.
  Multiplication and division / Rebecca Wingard-Nelson.
     p. cm. — (Ace your math test)
  Includes index.
  Summary: "Learn the basics of multiplication and division, and how to multiply and divide
by multiples of ten, larger numbers, and decimals and fractions"—Provided by publisher.
  ISBN 978-0-7660-3779-3
  1. Multiplication—Juvenile literature. 2. Division—Juvenile literature. I. Title.
  QA115.W7537 2011
  513.2'13—dc22
                               2011002101

Paperback ISBN 978-1-4644-0006-3
ePUB ISBN 978-1-4645-0456-3
PDF ISBN 978-1-4646-0456-0

Printed in the United States of America

092011 Lake Book Manufacturing, Inc., Melrose Park, IL

10 9 8 7 6 5 4 3 2 1

To Our Readers: We have done our best to make sure all Internet Addresses in this book
were active and appropriate when we went to press. However, the author and the publisher
have no control over and assume no liability for the material available on those Internet sites
or on other Web sites they may link to. Any comments or suggestions can be sent by e-mail
to comments@enslow.com or to the address on the back cover.

♻ Enslow Publishers, Inc., is committed to printing our books on recycled paper. The paper
in every book contains 10% to 30% post-consumer waste (PCW). The cover board on the
outside of each book contains 100% PCW. Our goal is to do our part to help young people
and the environment too!

Illustration Credits: Shutterstock.com

Cover Photos: Shutterstock.com

CONTENTS

Test-Taking Tips

Be Prepared!

Most of the topics that are found on math tests are taught in the classroom. Paying attention in class, taking good notes, and keeping up with your homework are the best ways to be prepared for tests.

Practice

Use test preparation materials, such as flash cards and timed worksheets, to practice your basic math skills. Take practice tests. They show the kinds of items that will be on the actual test. They can show you what areas you understand, and what areas you need more practice in.

Test Day!

The Night Before

Relax. Eat a good meal. Go to bed early enough to get a good night's sleep. Don't cram on new material! Review the material you know is going to be on the test.

Get what you need ready. Sharpen your pencils, set out things like erasers, a calculator, and any extra materials, like books, protractors, tissues, or cough drops.

The Big Day

Get up early enough to eat breakfast and not have to hurry. Wear something that is comfortable and makes you feel good. Listen to your favorite music.

Get to school and class on time. Stay calm. Stay positive.

Test Time!

Before you begin, take a deep breath. Focus on the test, not the people or things around you. Remind yourself to do your best, and not worry about what you do not know.

Work through the entire test, but don't spend too much time on any one problem. Don't rush, but move quickly, answering all of the questions you can do easily. Go back a second time and answer the questions that take more time.

Read each question completely. Read all the answer choices. Eliminate answers that are obviously wrong. Read word problems carefully, and decide what the problem is asking.

Check each answer to make sure it is reasonable. Estimate numbers to see if your answer makes sense.

Concentrate on the test. Stay focused. If your attention starts to wander, take a short break. Breathe. Relax. Refocus. Don't get upset if you can't answer a question. Mark it, then come back to it later.

When you finish, look back over the entire test. Are all of the questions answered? Check as many problems as you can. Look at your calculations and make sure you have the same answer on the blank as you do on your worksheet.

Let's Go!

Three common types of test problems are covered in this book: Multiple Choice, Show Your Work, and Explain Your Answer. Tips on how to solve each, as well as common errors to avoid, are also presented. Knowing what to expect on a test and what is expected of you will have you ready to ace every math test you take.

1. Basic Facts

Repeated Addition

Multiplication adds the same number over and over. For example, multiplying 4 by 3 is the same as adding 4 three times. ($4 \times 3 = 4 + 4 + 4$)

Definitions

factor: A number that is multiplied in a multiplication problem.

product: The result of multiplying numbers.

$$\text{factor} \times \text{factor} = \text{product}$$

The cost of a ticket to the junior high dance is $5. What is the cost of three tickets?

The problem can be solved in two ways.

Use addition: Add the cost of each ticket. Each is $5. Add $5 three times.

$$\$5 + \$5 + \$5 = \$15$$

Use multiplication: Multiply the cost of each ticket by the number of tickets.

$$\$5 \times 3 = \$15$$

TEST TIME: Multiple Choice

What is the product of 6 and 2?

a. 8
b. 10
c. 12
d. 13

When you can know the answer to a multiple choice question or you can solve it easily, mark the answer.

This problem multiplies 6 by 2. A number multiplied by two is the same as adding the number to itself, or doubling it. 6 + 6 = 12

Solution: The correct answer is c.

Test-Taking Hint

Multiple choice questions give you a set of answers. You choose which of the given answers is correct.

Basic Facts

Memorizing the basic multiplication facts for factors 1 through 12 will help you multiply larger numbers. Some tips can help you memorize the facts.

Tips

Count By: Any multiplication fact can be found by counting by one of the factors. For 5×3, count by 5 three times: 5, 10, 15. So, $5 \times 3 = 15$.

Doubles: A number multiplied by 2 is double the original number. For 8×2, double 8 is 16. So, $8 \times 2 = 16$.

Double-double: A number multiplied by 4 is double-double the original number. For example, to solve 3×4, first double 3 to 6. Double 6 is 12. So, $3 \times 4 = 12$.

Add one more: When you know some multiplication facts, you can find others by adding one more. If you know that $11 \times 6 = 66$, you can add one more 6 to find 12×6. Since $66 + 6 = 72$, then $12 \times 6 = 72$.

Nines: The digits in the products for the nines multiplication facts from 1 to 10 have a sum of 9. For $9 \times 7 = 63$, add the digits in 63: $6 + 3 = 9$.

Fives: A product of 5 and another number always ends in 0 or 5. For example, $5 \times 3 = 15$ and $5 \times 8 = 40$.

Even factors: A product of an even number and another number is always even. For example, $4 \times 6 = 24$.

TEST TIME: Show Your Work

Complete the multiplication table.

	1	2	3	4	5	6
1	1	2	3	4	5	6
2	2	4	(6)	8	10	12
3	3	6	9	12	15	18
4	4	8	12	16	20	24
5	5	10	15	20	25	30
6	6	12	18	24	30	36

A multiplication table has one set of factors along the top and one set of factors along the left side. Each cell is filled with the product of the factors for that row and column.

For each empty cell, find the factor for that row and multiply it by the factor for that column. For example, the cell with the red circle has a row factor of 2 and a column factor of 3. $2 \times 3 = 6$.

Test-Taking Hint

Questions that do not give you solutions to choose from are sometimes called "Show Your Work" questions. You may need to fill in a blank or you may need to show how you got your answer.

2. Powers and Multiples of Ten

Definitions

power of ten: A number that begins with a one and is followed by zeros. The numbers 10, 100, and 1,000 are powers of ten. Powers of ten are products of 10 multiplied by itself. 10 to the third power is $10 \times 10 \times 10 = 1,000$.

multiples of ten: Products of 10 multiplied by another number. The number 80 is a multiple of ten because $10 \times 8 = 80$. All multiples of ten end in a zero.

Multiplication by a Power of Ten

Multiply 6 by 10, 100, and 1,000.

Step 1: To find the product of a power of ten and another number, add the same number of zeros to the other factor as there are in the power of ten.

To multiply by 10, add one zero.	$6 \times 10 = 60$
To multiply by 100, add two zeros.	$6 \times 100 = 600$
To multiply by 1,000, add three zeros.	$6 \times 1,000 = 6,000$

TEST TIME: Multiple Choice

What is the product of 30 and 100?

        a. 30
        b. 300
       (c.) 3,000
        d. 30,000

To multiply a number by 100, add two zeros. When you put two zeros to the right of 30, you get 3,000.

Solution: The correct answer is c.

Test-Taking Hint

Mark your answers clearly. On tests that have circles to fill in, make sure you are neat and fill in the full circle.

Multiples of Ten

Marcos had 20 rabbits that he sold for $30 each. What was the total selling price of all the rabbits?

Step 1: Decide what operation must be performed. There are 20 rabbits that are sold for $30 each. Multiply 20 by 30.

$$20 \times 30 = \underline{}$$

Step 2: Numbers that end in zero can be multiplied by removing the zeros first. In this problem, each factor ends in zero. Remove the zeros.

$$2 \times 3 = \underline{}$$

Step 3: Multiply the basic fact that is left.

$$2 \times 3 = 6$$

Step 4: Add the same number of zeros to the right side of the product as you removed in Step 2. You removed two zeros, so add two zeros to the right of the product.

$$20 \times 30 = 600$$

The total selling price for all of the rabbits was $600.

TEST TIME: Explain Your Answer

How are multiplying by powers of ten and multiplying by multiples of ten similar?

Solution: When you multiply by a power or multiple of ten, you can first ignore the zeros on the right and multiply the basic fact.

For a power of ten problem, the basic fact is a ones fact.

In the problem 8×100, the basic fact is $8 \times 1 = 8$.

So, $8 \times 100 = 800$.

In a multiple of ten problem, the basic fact is not a ones fact.

In the problem 70×5, the basic fact is $7 \times 5 = 35$.

So, $70 \times 5 = 350$.

Test-Taking Hint

Some problems ask a question and ask you to explain your answer. Others just ask for an explanation. Your score is based on both a correct response and how clearly you explain your reasoning. If there is no direct computation, try to include an example when you can.

3. Multiplication Properties

The Zero Product Property

Multiply *0 × 9 and 82 × 0.*

Step 1: Multiply 0 × 9.

$$0 \times 9 = 0$$

Step 2: Multiply 82 × 0.

$$82 \times 0 = 0$$

Any number multiplied by zero has a product of zero.

The Property of One

Multiply *1 × 7 and 68 × 1.*

Step 1: Multiply 1 × 7.

$$1 \times 7 = 7$$

Step 2: Multiply 68 × 1.

$$68 \times 1 = 68$$

Any number multiplied by one has a product of itself.

Which of the following illustrates the Associative Property?

    a. $3 \times (2 \times 4) = (3 \times 2) \times 4$

    b. $2 \times 45 = 45 \times 2$

    c. $1 \times 16 = 16$

    d. $3 \times 0 = 0$

The associative property says that when you multiply more than two numbers, changing the grouping of the factors does not change the product. Answers a and b show how factors can be moved or grouped and have the same value. Answer a keeps the same order, but groups the factors differently. Answer b changes the order of the factors.

Solution: The correct answer is a.

Test-Taking Hint

When a question is taking an especially long time or has you stumped, leave the question and go on. Come back later if you have time. Another question may give you a clue that can help you solve the problem.

TEST TIME: Explain Your Answer

Explain the commutative property of multiplication using an example.
How can it help you memorize basic multiplication facts?

Solution: The commutative property of multiplication allows the order of factors in a multiplication problem to be changed without changing the product. For example,

$$4 \times 8 = 32 \text{ and } 8 \times 4 = 32.$$

The commutative property lets you learn two basic facts at once. When you know one fact, you also know the fact for the factors in the other order. When you know 4×8, you also know 8×4.

Three Factors

The associative property can be used to group factors so that problems are easier to solve.

Use mental multiplication to find the product of 8 × 2 × 3.

Step 1: Think:

The associative property tells me I can group the factors in any order. I can multiply 8 and 2, or 2 and 3 first.

$$(8 \times 2) \times 3 = 8 \times (2 \times 3)$$
$$16 \quad \times 3 = 8 \times \quad 6$$

Step 2: Think:

If I multiply the 8 by 2 first, then I need to multiply 16 by 3.
If I multiply the 2 by 3 first, then I need to multiply 8 by 6.
8 × 6 is a basic fact. 8 × 6 = 48

$$8 \times 2 \times 3 = 48$$

Test-Taking Hint

Know math definitions and know the reasoning behind the math.

4. The Distributive Property

Use the Property

Show more than one way to solve 6 × (9 + 5).

The distributive property can be used when one of the factors in a multiplication problem is written as a sum. The distributive property says you can find the sum first, then multiply. Or you can multiply by each addend separately, then add the products. The answer is the same.

Step 1: You can add inside the parentheses first, then multiply

$$6 \times (9 + 5) = 6 \times (14)$$

Step 2: You can distribute the 6 and multiply, then add the products.

$$6 \times (9 + 5) = (6 \times 9) + (6 \times 5) = (54) + (30) = 84$$

TEST TIME: Explain Your Answer

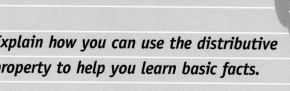

Explain how you can use the distributive property to help you learn basic facts.

Solution:

When you know the basic facts for some numbers, you can use what you know to learn the basic facts for other numbers. Let's look at an example.

Multiply 8 × 7.

8 × 7 = 8 × (5 + 2)	If you don't know the basic facts for 7's, you can break 7 into 5 + 2.
	Use the distributive property to "distribute"
(8 × 5) + (8 × 2)	each addend.
(40) + (16)	Multiply.
56	Then add.
8 × 7 = 56	

TEST TIME: Multiple Choice

Which expression has the same value as (10 × 2) + (7 × 2)?

a. 12 × 14
b. 17 × 2
c. 12 + 9
d. 17 × 4

The distributive property tells you that when two numbers are each multiplied by the same number and then added, you can add them first, then do the multiplication. In this expression, both 10 and 7 are first being multiplied by 2, and then added. You can add 10 + 7, then multiply by 2.

Solution: The correct answer is b.

Subtraction

The distributive property can also be used with subtraction.

How can the facts for 10s be used to learn the facts for 9s?

Step 1: You can use a subtraction fact to get from 10 to 9.

$$10 - 1 = 9$$

Step 2: Choose a 9s fact to use as an example.

Let's choose 9 × 8.

Step 3: Replace 9 with the expression 10 − 1.

$$9 \times 8 = (10 - 1) \times 8$$

Step 4: Use the distributive property.

$$9 \times 8 = (10 \times 8) - (1 \times 8)$$

Step 5: Do the math.

$$9 \times 8 = (10 \times 8) - (1 \times 8)$$
$$= (80) - (8)$$
$$= 72$$

9 × 8 = 72

5. Use the Facts

Multi-digit Multiplication

Any number can be multiplied by a one-digit number using place value and basic facts.

Use place value to multiply 21 × 4.

Step 1: Write the problem in a column to help keep track of the place value.

$$\begin{array}{r} 21 \\ \times\ 4 \\ \hline \end{array}$$

Step 2: Multiply the digit in the ones place, 1, by the factor 4. 1 × 4 = 4. Write a 4 in the ones place of the product.

$$\begin{array}{r} 21 \\ \times\ 4 \\ \hline 4 \end{array}$$

Step 3: Multiply the digit in the tens place, 2, by the factor 4. 2 × 4 = 8. Write an 8 in the tens place of the product.

$$\begin{array}{r} 21 \\ \times\ 4 \\ \hline 84 \end{array}$$

21 × 4 = 84

TEST TIME: Show Your Work

Hilda made 32 ounces of lemonade in each of 3 pitchers. How many ounces of lemonade did she make in all?

Find the amount of lemonade she made in all by multiplying the amount in each pitcher by the number of pitchers.
Multiply each place in the factor 32 by 3.

$$
\begin{array}{r}
32 \\
\times\ 3 \\
\hline
96
\end{array}
$$

Write the answer in a full sentence.

Solution: Hilda made 96 ounces of lemonade in all.

Test-Taking Hint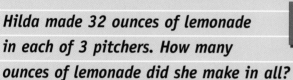

Word problems, or story problems, should be answered in complete sentences.

TEST TIME: Multiple Choice

What is the product of 321 and 2?

a. 323

b. 620

c. 642

d. 864

This problem can be solved in a number of ways. You could double 321, since the other factor is 2. You could multiply using place value. Or, you can use what you know about multiplication to eliminate wrong answers.

Multiply only the ones place. $2 \times 1 = 2$.
Eliminate any answers that do not have a 2 in the ones place.

Solution: Since answers a, b, and d are incorrect, the correct answer is c.

Use one of the other methods to check the answer.
$321 + 321 = 642$

Partial Products

Use partial products to solve 33 × 2.

Step 1: The distributive property tells you that you can separate the factors into parts. Partial products are the results of multiplying part of one factor by the other factor.

Use the distributive property to separate 33 into 30 + 3.

33 × 2 is the same as (30 + 3) × 2

Step 2: Multiply each addend.

$$(30 + 3) \times 2 = (30 \times 2) + (3 \times 2)$$
$$= \quad 60 \quad + \quad 6$$

Step 3: Add the partial products.

$$60 + 6 = 66$$

33 × 2 = 66

Test-Taking Hint

Some multiple choice questions can be solved by eliminating choices that are obviously incorrect.

6. Regrouping

Partial Products

Sometimes the partial product from one place will carry over into the next place.

Use partial products to multiply 28 × 4.

Step 1: Use the distributive property to separate 28 into 20 + 8.

> **28 × 4 is the same as (20 + 8) × 4**

Step 2: Multiply each addend.

$$(20 + 8) \times 4 = (20 \times 4) + (8 \times 4)$$
$$= \quad 80 \quad + \quad 32$$

Step 3: Add the partial products. In this problem, the product of the factors from the ones place carries into the tens place. When the digits from the tens places are added, the sum carries into the hundreds place.

$$
\begin{array}{r}
80 \\
+ \ 32 \\
\hline
112
\end{array}
$$

28 × 4 = 112

Which of the following expressions has the same value as 85 × 5?

a. (80 + 5) × 5
b. (80 × 5) + (5 × 5)
c. (400) + (25)
d. All of the above

Each of the expressions in answers a, b, and c are steps that use the distributive property on the original expression. None of the steps change the value, so all three are correct.

Solution: Answer d is correct.

Test-Taking Hint

In multiple choice problems with the answer choice all of the above, it is best to check all of the choices.

Regrouping

Multiply 43 × 7.

Step 1: Write the problem in a column.
Line up the digits by their place value.

$$\begin{array}{r} 43 \\ \times\ 7 \\ \hline \end{array}$$

Step 2: Multiply the ones. 7 × 3 = 21. The 21 ones regroups as 2 tens and 1 one. Write a 1 in the ones place. Carry the 2 to the tens place.

$$\begin{array}{r} 2 \\ 43 \\ \times\ 7 \\ \hline 1 \end{array}$$

Step 3: Multiply the tens. 7 × 4 = 28. Add the 2 tens you carried from the ones place. 28 + 2 = 30. The 30 tens regroups as 3 hundreds and 0 tens. Write a 0 in the tens place. Write a 3 in the hundreds place.

$$\begin{array}{r} 2 \\ 43 \\ \times\ 7 \\ \hline 301 \end{array}$$

43 × 7 = 301

TEST TIME: Show Your Work

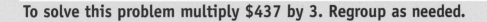

The Walker family has 3 children who are all going to summer camp. The cost is $437 per child. How much will it cost in all?

To solve this problem multiply $437 by 3. Regroup as needed.

Solution:

$$
\begin{array}{r}
12 \\
\$\,437 \\
\times\ \ 3 \\
\hline
\$1{,}311
\end{array}
$$

It will cost the Walker family $1,311 to send all three children to camp.

Test-Taking Hint

Calculators are useful tools for solving and checking the solutions to math problems. Try checking the answer to the Walker family problem on a calculator.

7. Multiplying by Two Digits

Use Two Steps

What is the product of 52 × 14?

Step 1: Multiplying a number by two digits can be done in two steps. Use the distributive property to separate the second factor into tens and ones, 10 + 4.

Multiply the first factor, 52, only by the ones, 4.

$$\begin{array}{r} 52 \\ \times\ 4 \\ \hline 208 \end{array}$$

Step 2: Multiply the first factor by the tens of the second factor, 10. Ten is a power of ten. You can put a zero in the ones place of the answer and multiply 52 by 1.

$$\begin{array}{r} 52 \\ \times\ 10 \\ \hline 520 \end{array}$$

Step 3: Add the partial products.

$$\begin{array}{r} 208 \\ +\ 520 \\ \hline 728 \end{array}$$

52 × 14 = 728

TEST TIME: Explain Your Answer

Explain how you can use expanded notation to multiply numbers with more than one digit.

Solution: Expanded notation separates a multi-digit number by place value. For example, 647 in expanded notation is 600 + 40 + 7.

To multiply any number by a multi-digit number, you can write each number in expanded notation. Use the distributive property to multiply each part of each factor.

46 × 72 can be multiplied using the expanded forms: 40 + 6 and 70 + 2.

$$46 \times 72 = (40 + 6) \times (70 + 2)$$

Distribute the first factor to each part of the second factor.

$$= (40 + 6)(70) \qquad + (40 + 6)(2)$$

Distribute again. $= (40)(70) + (6)(70) + (40)(2) + (6)(2)$

Multiply. $= (2,800) + (420) + (80) + (12)$

Add. $= 3,312$

$$46 \times 72 = 3,312$$

Columns

What is the product of 64 × 23?

Step 1: Write the problem in a column.

$$
\begin{array}{r}
64 \\
\times\ 23 \\
\hline
\end{array}
$$

Step 2: Multiply the first factor, 64, by the ones of the second factor, 3.

$$
\begin{array}{r}
\cancel{1} \\
64 \\
\times\ 23 \\
\hline
192 \\
\end{array}
$$

Step 3: Multiply the first factor, 64, by the tens of the second factor, 2. Write the partial product from the tens below the partial product from the ones. Write a zero in the ones place first since you are actually multiplying by 20, not 2.

$$
\begin{array}{r}
\cancel{1} \\
64 \\
\times\ 23 \\
\hline
192 \\
1,280 \\
\end{array}
$$

Step 3: Add the partial products.

$$
\begin{array}{r}
\cancel{1} \\
64 \\
\times\ 23 \\
\hline
192 \\
+\ 1,280 \\
\hline
1,472 \\
\end{array}
$$

64 × 23 = 1,472

TEST TIME: Multiple Choice

A school fund-raiser sold boxes of popcorn. Each box contained 32 microwave bags. How many bags of popcorn were sold if there were 126 boxes sold?

a. 3,922
b. 4,022
c. 4,032
d. 4,132

To solve this problem, multiply the number of boxes sold by the number of bags in each box.

$$
\begin{array}{r}
\cancel{x} \\
126 \\
\times\ 32 \\
\hline
252 \\
+\ 3780 \\
\hline
4,032
\end{array}
$$

Solution: Answer c is correct.

Test-Taking Hint

An answer in a multiple choice problem might look correct if you go too quickly. Often the wrong answers listed are ones you would find if you made a common error.

8. Multiplying Larger Numbers

Greater Number Multiplication

For a full year, 365 days, Jace drank a bottle of soda each day. Each bottle contains 245 calories. How many calories did Jace consume from the soda in that year?

Step 1: To solve this problem, multiply the number of days Jace drank the soda, 365, by the number of calories in each bottle, 245. Write the problem in a column.

$$\begin{array}{r} 365 \\ \times\ 245 \\ \hline \end{array}$$

Step 2: Multiply the first factor, 365, by the ones of the second factor, 5.

$$\begin{array}{r} 32 \\ 365 \\ \times\ 245 \\ \hline 1825 \end{array}$$

Step 3: Multiply the first factor, 365, by the tens of the second factor, 4. Write the partial product from the tens below the partial product from the ones. Write a zero in the ones place first since you are actually multiplying by 40, not 4.

```
 2̶2̶
 3̶2̶
 365
× 245
 1825
14600
```

Step 4: Multiply the first factor, 365, by the hundreds of the second factor, 2. Write the partial product from the hundreds below the partial product from the tens. Write two zeros in the ones and tens place first since you are actually multiplying by 200, not 2.

```
  1̶1̶
  2̶2̶
  3̶2̶
  365
× 245
 1825
14600
73000
```

Step 3: Add the partial products.

```
   365
 × 245
  1825
 14600
+ 73000
 89,425
```

Jace consumed 89,425 calories in soda that year.

TEST TIME: Show Your Work

Use expanded notation to multiply 324 × 111.

This problem asks you to use expanded notation to do the multiplication. Include your work in your answer.

Solution:

$$324 \times 111 = 324 \times (100 + 10 + 1)$$
$$= (324 \times 100) + (324 \times 10) + (324 \times 1)$$
$$= (32,400) + (3,240) + (324)$$
$$= 35,964$$

$$324 \times 111 = 35,964$$

TEST TIME: Multiple Choice

Tickets to a benefit concert were sold on Friday and Saturday for $160 each. On Friday, there were 1,246 tickets sold. On Saturday, another 2,119 tickets were sold. How much money was collected in all for the tickets?

> a. $53,840
> b. $199,360
> c. $339,040
> d. $538,400

This problem can be solved in two steps.
Use a calculator to add Friday and Saturday's ticket sales.
1,246 + 2,119 = 3,365

Use the calculator again to multiply the total sales by the cost of each ticket.
3,365 × $160 = $538,400

Solution: Answer d is correct.

Test-Taking Hint

Some tests allow you to use calculators. Use a calculator when you know how to solve a problem. It will save you time that you may need for other problems.

Definition

decimal: A number based on ten. In a decimal, a decimal point separates whole number values from values less than one.

16.23
whole number.less than one

Decimals and Whole Numbers

Decimals are multiplied in the same way as whole numbers.

Multiply 3 × 1.2.

Step 1: Ignore the decimal point and multiply as if both factors are whole numbers.

$$3 \times 1.2 = \underline{}$$
$$3 \times 12 = 36$$

Step 2: Count the number of decimal places after the decimal point in both factors.

3 has 0 decimal places. 1.2 has 1 decimal place.
There is 1 total decimal place.

Step 3: The total number of decimal places in the factors tells the number of decimal places in the product. Count one decimal place from the right. Place the decimal point in the answer.

$$3 \times 1.2 = 3.6$$

Teri earns $8.50 per hour. If she worked
9 hours in one day, how much did she earn?

        a. $70.50
        b. $72.00
        c. $76.50
        d. $81.50

The word *per* in this problem tells you to use multiplication.
You can quickly eliminate answers a and b by understanding that
$8.50 is greater than $8.00, so $8.50 × 9 is greater than $72.00.

Multiply using either a calculator or a paper and pencil.
$8.50 × 9 = $76.50.

Solution: The correct answer is c.

Test-Taking Hint

Be careful to avoid careless answers on easy questions.
Focus on each problem, and don't be in a hurry.

TEST TIME: Show Your Work

A picture is 4.2 inches long and 6.1 inches wide. What is the area of the picture?

The area of a rectangle is found by multiplying the length by the width. To multiply two decimals, multiply as if they are whole numbers. Count the number of decimal points in both factors. This is the number of decimal places in the product.

Solution:

$$
\begin{array}{r}
4.2 \text{ inches} \\
\times\ 6.1 \text{ inches} \\
\hline
42 \\
+\ 2520 \\
\hline
25.62
\end{array}
$$

The area of the picture is 25.62 square inches.

Test-Taking Hint

Remember to include the units in your answers. Area problems always have square units.

TEST TIME: Explain Your Answer

Multiply 8.4 by 10, by 100, and by 1,000. Explain any patterns you see.

Solution:

$8.4 \times 10 = 84$

$8.4 \times 100 = 840$

$8.4 \times 1,000 = 8,400$

In each equation, the digits stayed the same. The only difference was the location of the decimal point. For each zero in the power of ten, the decimal point moved one place to the right.

10. Multiplying Fractions

Fractions and Fractions

Fractions are multiplied in two steps.

Multiply 1/3 × 1/3.

Step 1: Multiply the numerators.

$$\frac{1}{3} \times \frac{1}{3} = \frac{1 \times 1}{} = \frac{1}{}$$

Step 2: Multiply the denominators.

$$\frac{1}{3} \times \frac{1}{3} = \frac{1 \times 1}{3 \times 3} = \frac{1}{9}$$

Multiply 1/2 × 5/8.

Step 1: Multiply the numerators.

$$\frac{1}{2} \times \frac{5}{8} = \frac{1 \times 5}{} = \frac{5}{}$$

Step 2: Multiply the denominators.

$$\frac{1}{2} \times \frac{5}{8} = \frac{1 \times 5}{2 \times 8} = \frac{5}{16}$$

TEST TIME: Show Your Work

You want to make 1/3 of a batch of
cupcakes. A one-batch recipe calls for 3/4 cup of butter.
How much butter do you need to make the cupcakes?

To make a fraction of a batch, you need to use a fraction of each
ingredient. To make 1/3 of a batch of cupcakes, you need 1/3 of
3/4 cup of butter.

$$1/3 \text{ of } 3/4 \text{ cup} = 1/3 \times 3/4$$

Multiply numerators.
Multiply denominators.

$$\frac{1 \times 3}{3 \times 4} = \frac{3}{12}$$

Reduce to lowest terms.

$$\frac{3}{12} = \frac{1}{4}$$

Solution: You need 1/4 cup of butter to make the cupcakes.

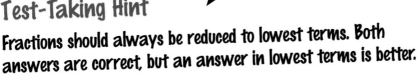

Test-Taking Hint

Fractions should always be reduced to lowest terms. Both
answers are correct, but an answer in lowest terms is better.

simplifying: Reducing fractions before you multiply.
Simplification makes the numbers smaller and easier to multiply.
It also saves you from needing to reduce the fractions later.

Whole Numbers and Fractions

Multiply 20 and 2/5.

Step 1: Write the whole number as an improper fraction with a denominator of 1.

$$\frac{20}{1} \times \frac{2}{5}$$

Step 2: Simplify by dividing the numerator of one fraction and the denominator of the other by a common factor. In this problem, you can divide 20 by 5, and 5 by 5.

$$\frac{\overset{4}{\cancel{20}}}{1} \times \frac{2}{\underset{1}{\cancel{5}}}$$

Step 3: Multiply the numerators and multiply the denominators.

$$\frac{4}{1} \times \frac{2}{1} = \frac{4 \times 2}{1 \times 1} = \frac{8}{1} = 8$$

TEST TIME: Multiple Choice

Tom drove an average speed of 60 miles per hour for $3 \frac{1}{6}$ hours. How many miles did Tom drive?

a. 130 miles
b. 166 miles
c. 190 miles
d. 210 miles

To find the distance Tom drove, multiply the number of hours he drove by the number of miles he drove per hour.

One way to solve this problem is to convert the whole number and the mixed fraction into improper fractions.

$$60 \times 3 \frac{1}{6} = \frac{\overset{10}{\cancel{60}}}{1} \times \frac{19}{\cancel{6}_1} = \frac{10}{1} \times \frac{19}{1} = \frac{190}{1} = 190$$

Solution: Answer c is correct.

Test-Taking Hint

When you finish your test, look it over and make sure you have answered every question.

11. Estimation: Multiplication

Rounding

Estimate the product of 614 and 581.

Step 1: One way to estimate a product of two numbers is to round each number, then multiply. Round each number to the hundreds place.

> **614 rounds to 600**
> **581 rounds to 600**

Step 2: Multiply using mental math. Each factor is a multiple of ten. Remove the zeros and find the basic fact.

> **$6 \times 6 = 36$, so**
> **$600 \times 600 = 360,000$**

614×581 is about 360,000

The actual product of 614 and 581 is 356,734.
360,000 is close to 356,734. This is a good estimate.

TEST TIME: Multiple Choice

Which of the following is NOT a good reason to estimate?
- a. Because you don't need an exact answer.
- b. Because you don't want to solve the problem.
- c. To predict what the answer might be.
- d. To check if an answer is reasonable.

This problem asks you to decide which reason is NOT a good one to find an estimate.

When you don't need an exact answer, to predict the answer, and to check if your answer is reasonable are all good reasons to estimate. To estimate because you don't want to solve a problem is NOT a good reason to estimate.

Solution: The correct answer is b.

Test-Taking Hint

Not all of the questions on a math test need computations. Know math definitions and know the reasons behind the math.

TEST TIME: Explain Your Answer

Linda is making 8 place mats. Each place mat uses 4/9 of a yard of fabric. Should Linda overestimate or underestimate to find the amount of fabric to buy? Why? About how much fabric should she buy?

This problem asks three questions. Be sure to answer each in your solution. An overestimate is a little larger than the exact solution. An underestimate is a little smaller than the exact solution.

Solution: When you need to be sure you have enough of something, like money, or in this case fabric, you should overestimate. To overestimate, make the fraction 4/9 a little larger, to 1/2.

Linda needs 8 place mats, each using about 1/2 of a yard of fabric. 8 × 1/2 = 4.

Linda should purchase about 4 yards of fabric.

Round to Whole Numbers

One way to estimate the answer to a problem that uses decimals or mixed fractions is to round each factor to the nearest whole number.

Estimate the product of 18 $\frac{1}{3}$ and 39 $\frac{3}{4}$.

Step 1: Find the nearest whole number to each mixed fraction.

$18 \frac{1}{3}$ rounds to **18.** $39 \frac{3}{4}$ rounds to **40.**

Step 2: Multiply the whole numbers.

$$18 \times 40 = 720$$

The product of $18\frac{1}{3}$ and $39\frac{3}{4}$ is about 720.

The exact answer to this problem is 728 $\frac{3}{4}$. 720 is a good estimate.

12. Division

How Many Groups?

Division lets you take an amount and separate it into equal smaller groups. Division can find the number of smaller groups or the size of each group.

How many groups of 4 coins can you make from 12 coins?

Step 1: One way to look at division is that it is repeated subtraction. How many times can you subtract 4 from 12? Start with 12, and subtract 4 at a time.

$$12 - 4 = 8$$
$$8 - 4 = 4$$
$$4 - 4 = 0$$

You can make 3 groups of 4 coins each from 12 coins.

TEST TIME: Multiple Choice

Which number is equivalent to 20/4?

a. 2

b. 3

c. 4

d. 5

A fraction is written as a whole number using division. Divide 20 into groups of 4. How many groups do you have? Use a sketch to help you. Draw 20, then separate 20 into groups of 4.

There are 5 groups.

Solution: The correct answer is d.

Test-Taking Hint

The fraction bar represents division.

10/2 is the same as 10 ÷ 2.

Size of Each Group?

When you know the size of the original group and you know the number of smaller equal groups, division can tell you the size of each smaller group.

How many objects are in each group if you divide 8 objects into 2 equal groups?

Step 1: You can show division using manipulatives. You can use 8 small objects. Put one object at a time into each of two groups until all of them are in a group.

Step 2: Count the number in each group. There are 4 objects in each group.

If 8 objects are put into two equal groups, there are 4 objects in each group.

Test-Taking Hint

Division is a quick way to repeatedly subtract the same amount.

TEST TIME: Show Your Work

A 30-ounce cheesecake is cut into 5-ounce slices. How many slices of cheesecake are there?

Problems that take one large item and split it into equal pieces are division problems.

Start with 30 ounces. Take 5 ounces away at a time until all 30 are gone.

Solution:

30 − 5 = 25   25 − 5 = 20   20 − 5 = 15

15 − 5 = 10   10 − 5 = 5   5 − 5 = 0

There are 6 slices of cheesecake.

13. Inverse Operations

Multiplication and Division

Inverse operations do the opposite of each other. Addition and subtraction are inverse operations. Multiplication and division are inverse operations.

What is the fact family that includes 3 × 2 = 6?

Step 1: For every multiplication fact, there is a related division fact. Multiplication combines 3 groups of 2 into 6. Division takes 6 and divides it into 2 groups of 3. When you know $3 \times 2 = 6$, you also know $6 \div 2 = 3$.

$$3 \times 2 = 6 \qquad 6 \div 2 = 3$$

Step 2: The commutative property tells you that since $3 \times 2 = 6$, then $2 \times 3 = 6$. The related division fact for $2 \times 3 = 6$ is $6 \div 3 = 2$.

$$2 \times 3 = 6 \qquad 6 \div 3 = 2$$

Step 3: The four related facts are sometimes called a fact family. Let's write them together.

$$3 \times 2 = 6 \qquad 6 \div 2 = 3$$
$$2 \times 3 = 6 \qquad 6 \div 3 = 2$$

TEST TIME: Multiple Choice

What is the missing number in this fact family?

$$6 \times \underline{} = 42 \qquad \underline{} \times 6 = 42$$
$$42 \div 6 = \underline{} \qquad 42 \div \underline{} = 6$$

a. 6
ⓑ 7
c. 8
d. 9

You can use any of the four facts to find the missing number. In each fact, the missing number is 7.

Solution: The correct answer is b.

The Multiplication Table

The multiplication table can help you find the answer to division problems.

Divide 24 ÷ 4.

Step 1: The divisor is 4. To divide using the multiplication table, find the column for the number you are dividing by, 4.

Step 2: The dividend is 24. Follow the column down to the number being divided, 24.

Step 3: Move left across the row that includes 24. This is the row for the factor 6. The quotient is 6.

	1	2	3	4	5	6
1	1	2	3	4	5	6
2	2	4	6	8	10	12
3	3	6	9	12	15	18
4	4	8	12	16	20	24
5	5	10	15	20	25	30
6	6	12	18	24	30	36
7	7	14	21	28	35	42

24 ÷ 4 = 6

TEST TIME: Show Your Work

Jose made 28 tacos for his family of 7. How many tacos are there for each person?

This is a division problem. Jose has a number of tacos, 28, and is dividing them evenly among 7 people. You can use a multiplication table or you can use a multiplication fact that you know.

If you know the multiplication fact $4 \times 7 = 28$, you also know $28 \div 7 = 4$.

Solution: There are 4 tacos for each person.

Test-Taking Hint

Put a small mark next to answers you're not sure of or do not finish. When you finish your test, go back to those problems.

14. Division Facts

Division and One

Divide 12 ÷ 1.

Step 1: The multiplication property of one says that any number multiplied by 1 is itself. The same is true for division. Any number divided by 1 is itself.

$$12 \div 1 = 12$$

Does this make sense? Yes. If you start with a number of items, and put them all in one group, how many are in each group? All of them.

Divide 12 ÷ 12.

Step 1: Think of this in a problem. If you have 12 items, and you put them into 12 equal groups, how many are in each group? One.

$$12 \div 12 = 1$$

Any number divided by itself is one.

TEST TIME: Multiple Choice

$45 \div 0 = \_\_$?

        a. 0

        b. 1

        c. 45

        (d.) No answer

It is impossible to separate items into zero groups. Division by zero has no answer.

Solution: The correct answer is d.

Test-Taking Hint

Work at your own pace. Don't worry about how fast anyone else is taking the same test.

More Zeros

What is 0 divided by 10?

Step 1: If you begin with a total group of zero objects, no matter how many groups you make, each will have zero objects in it. Zero divided by any number is always zero.

$$0 \div 10 = 0$$

Test-Taking Hint

Read word problems carefully. Multiplication and division problems often use the same words.

Other Facts

What is 24 divided by 2?

Step 1: Dividing a number by 2 is the same as finding half of it. Half of 24 is 12.

$$24 \div 2 = 12$$

TEST TIME: Show Your Work

Cami has taken 3 math quizzes.
Each quiz is worth 10 points. Her scores are 7, 9, and 8.
What is Cami's average score?

Many words that show multiplication are also used to show division. The word "average" in this problem is asking you to divide. You can find the average by adding the quiz scores, then dividing by the number of quizzes.

Solution: $7 + 9 + 8 = 24$
$24 \div 3 = 8$

Cami's average score on the three quizzes is an 8.

Because multiplication and division are inverse operations, you can use multiplication to check division.
If Cami's average is an 8, multiply the average by the number of quizzes she has taken, 3. $\quad 8 \times 3 = 24$
Did she score 24 points in all? Yes.

15. Remainders

Uneven Division

Divide 7 ÷ 2.

Step 1: How many times can you take 2 from 7?

$$7 - 2 = 5$$
$$5 - 2 = 3$$
$$3 - 2 = 1$$

Step 2: You can take 2 from 7 three times. There is one left. One is the remainder. A remainder can be written using the letter R, usually a small uppercase.

$$3R1$$

A remainder may also be written as a fraction. The remainder is the numerator, and the divisor is the denominator.

$$3 \, ^1/_2$$

A remainder may also be written as a decimal. The decimal part is the remainder. The fraction 1/2 is the same as the decimal 0.5, so 3 1/2 is the same as 3.5

$$3.5$$

TEST TIME: Show Your Work

Divide 16 ÷ 3. Write the remainder as a fraction.

To solve this problem, find the basic multiplication fact for 3s that has the closest product to 16, without going over.

$3 \times 4 = 12$ $3 \times 5 = 15$ $3 \times 6 = 18$

The closest fact is $3 \times 5 = 15$, and $15 \div 3 = 5$. If you make 5 groups of 3 out of 16, you use 15, and have 1 left over. Write the remainder as a fraction. Remember, the denominator is the divisor.

Solution: $16 \div 3 = 5\frac{1}{3}$

Test-Taking Hint

Some problems ask for your answer to be in a certain form, like a fraction or a decimal. Read carefully!

Divisibility

Is 249 divisible by 3?

Step 1: If the sum of all of the digits in a multi-digit number is divisible by 3, then the number is divisible by 3. Add all of the digits.

$$249$$
$$2 + 4 + 9 = 15$$
$$15 \div 3 = 5$$

249 is divisible by 3.

Test-Taking Hint

You can use some clues to help you decide if a multi-digit number is divisible by certain numbers.

All even numbers are divisible by 2.

If the sum of the digits of a number is divisible by 3, the number is divisible by 3.

If the last 2 digits of a number are divisible by 4, it is divisible by 4.

If the last digit is a 0 or a 5, it is divisible by 5.

If the number is divisible by both 2 and 3, it is divisible by 6.

If the sum of the digits is divisible by 9, it is divisible by 9.

If the last digit is 0, the number is divisible by 10.

TEST TIME: Multiple Choice

Which of the following sets of numbers can divide into 240 evenly?

          a. 3, 4, 5, 9
          b. 2, 3, 4, 6, 10
          c. 1, 4, 8, 9, 10
          d. 2, 4, 6, 9

Try making a list. Decide which numbers between 1 and 10 will divide 240 evenly.

240 divides evenly by 1, 2, 3, 4, 5, 6, 8, and 10.

Answers a, c, and d all include 9, but 240 is not divisible by 9.

Solution: The correct answer is b.

16. Interpreting Remainders

Test-Taking Hint

In word problems with a remainder, the remainder may be interpreted in different ways. You may need to increase the quotient (as in the example below), drop the remainder, or use the remainder as the answer.

Increase the Quotient

Harriet is putting 38 cupcakes into boxes that will each hold 6 cupcakes. How many boxes does she need?

Step 1: This is a division problem. Divide the number of cupcakes by the number of cupcakes per box.

$$38 \div 6$$

Step 2: Find the closest multiplication fact for 6s without going over 38.

$$6 \times 6 = 36, \text{ so } 36 \div 6 = 6$$

There are 2 left over. $38 \div 6 = 6R2$

Step 3: Interpret the remainder. If 38 cupcakes fit into 6 boxes with 2 left over, you need one more box than 6.

Harriet needs 7 boxes.

TEST TIME: Multiple Choice

Branson needs to make 29 brownies. Each box of mix makes 12 brownies. How many boxes of mix does Branson need?

a. 1

b. 2

c. 3

d. 4

This is a division problem. Divide the number of brownies by the number of brownies per box. Since 29 is not divisible by 12, the closest multiplication fact without going over is 12 × 2 = 24. If you take 24 from 29, there are 5 left over. This means 2 boxes of mix will make 24 brownies, but Branson needs 29. He needs to make one more box.

Solution: The correct answer is c.

TEST TIME: Show Your Work

Ms. Thomas has 47 seeds to plant in her garden. She wants to plant the seeds in exact rows of 5. How many seeds will she have left over?

This is a division problem: 47 seeds are divided into rows of 5 seeds each.

Solution:
$5 \times 9 = 45$, so, $47 \div 5 = 9R2$

The problem asks for the number of seeds that are left over. This is the remainder.

There will be 2 seeds left over.

What does the quotient mean in terms of this word problem? The quotient is the number of rows. Ms. Thomas will have 9 rows of exactly 5 seeds. If she used the remaining seeds, she would have a 10th row with 2 seeds in the final row.

Drop the Remainder

There are 26 people standing in line to get on a roller coaster. Each seat holds 4 people. How many seats can be completely filled?

Step 1: This is a division problem. Divide the number of people in line by the number of people per seat.

$$26 \div 4 = \underline{\quad}$$

Step 2: The number 26 does not divide evenly by 4. Find the multiplication fact for 4s that has a product closest to 26 without going over.

$$4 \times 6 = 24, \text{ so } 24 \div 4 = 6$$

Step 3: If you take 6 groups of 4, 24, from 26, you have 6 full groups, and 2 left over.

$$26 \div 4 = 6R2$$

Step 4: Read the question again and decide how the answer to the division equation relates to the problem. There are 26 people in line. There are 6 seats with 4 people in each, and then there are 2 more people left over.

The problem asks for the number of completely filled seats.

6 seats can be completely filled.

Definition

long division: A method that uses place value to divide multi-digit numbers. Long division uses the long division symbol.

$$\text{divisor} \overline{) \text{dividend}}^{\text{quotient}}$$

Long Division

Divide 72 ÷ 3.

Step 1: Write the problem using the long division symbol.

$$3 \overline{) 72}$$

Step 2: Divide one place value at a time, beginning on the left. How many 3s can you take from 7? You can take 2. Write a 2 in the answer above the 7.

$$3 \overline{) 72}^{2}$$

Step 3: Multiply the number you wrote in the answer, 2, by the divisor, 3: 2 × 3 = 6. Write the product, 6, below the 7.

$$\begin{array}{r} 2 \\ 3 \overline{) 72} \\ 6 \end{array}$$

Step 4: Subtract: $7 - 6 = 1$.
Compare. The difference, 1, should be less than the divisor, 3.

$$\begin{array}{r} 2 \\ 3\overline{)\,72} \\ -6 \\ \hline 1 \end{array}$$

Step 5: Bring down the next digit, 2.

$$\begin{array}{r} 2 \\ 3\overline{)\,72} \\ -6\downarrow \\ \hline 12 \end{array}$$

Step 6: Divide the new number, 12, by the divisor, 3. $12 \div 3 = 4$.
Write a 4 above the 2 in the answer.

$$\begin{array}{r} 24 \\ 3\overline{)\,72} \\ -6 \\ \hline 12 \end{array}$$

Step 7: Multiply: $4 \times 3 = 12$.
Write 12 below the 12.

$$\begin{array}{r} 24 \\ 3\overline{)\,72} \\ -6 \\ \hline 12 \\ -12 \end{array}$$

Step 8: Subtract. There are no more numbers to bring down.

$$\begin{array}{r} 24 \\ 3\overline{)\,72} \\ -6 \\ \hline 12 \\ -12 \\ \hline 0 \end{array}$$

$72 \div 3 = 24$

TEST TIME: Show Your Work

Divide 77 ÷ 4.

Use long division. When there are no more numbers to bring down, the difference left is the remainder.

Solution:

```
        19R1
    4 ) 77
       − 4
        37
       − 36
         1
```

77 ÷ 4 = 19R1

Check division using multiplication. Multiply the answer by the divisor.

$$19 \times 4 = 76$$

Add the remainder to the product. 76 + 1 = 77.

The result should be the dividend.

TEST TIME: Multiple Choice

$314 \div 5 =$ _____

    a. 60R6

    (b.) 62R4

    c. 63R1

    d. 63R4

Use long division. When the digit in the first place is less than the divisor, begin with the first two digits.

$$
\begin{array}{r}
62\text{R}4 \\
5 \overline{)\ 314} \\
-30 \\
\hline
14 \\
-10 \\
\hline
4
\end{array}
$$

Solution: The correct answer is b.

Test-Taking Hint

Remember the steps to long division:

Divide, Multiply, Subtract, Compare, Bring down.

18. Dividing by Larger Numbers

Use Long Division

Divide 744 ÷ 24.

Step 1: Write the problem using the long division symbol.

$$24 \overline{) \, 744}$$

Step 2: Divide one place value at a time, beginning on the left. Can you take any 24s from 7? No. Can you take any 24s from 74? Yes.
Find the largest number of times you can take 24 from 74. Try to think of a close number, then check using multiplication.
Try 2: 24 × 2 = 48
Try 3: 24 × 3 = 72
You can take 3 groups of 24 from 74.
Write a 3 in the answer above the 4.

$$24 \overline{) \, 744}^{\,3}$$

Step 3: Multiply the number you wrote in the answer, 3, by the divisor, 24.
24 × 3 = 72

$$24 \overline{) \, 744}^{\,3}$$
$$\underline{72}$$

Step 4: Subtract: 74 − 72 = 2.
Compare. The difference, 2, should be less than the divisor, 24.

$$24 \overline{) \, 744}^{\,3}$$
$$\underline{-72}$$
$$2$$

Step 5: Bring down the next digit, 4.

$$
\begin{array}{r}
3 \\
24 \overline{)\ 744} \\
-72 \\
\hline
24
\end{array}
$$

Step 6: Repeat the steps.
Divide. Multiply. Subtract. Compare.
There are no more numbers to bring down.

$$
\begin{array}{r}
31 \\
24 \overline{)\ 744} \\
-72 \\
\hline
24 \\
-24 \\
\hline
0
\end{array}
$$

$744 \div 24 = 31$

Test-Taking Hint

Use the inverse operation to check your work.

Multiplication checks division.

Since $31 \times 24 = 744$, $744 \div 24 = 31$ is correct.

TEST TIME: Multiple Choice

Matt took a 15-day holiday and drove around the country visiting relatives. He drove a total of 3,210 miles. How many miles did he average per day?

a. 212
b. 214
c. 3,195
d. 48,150

When you understand this is a division problem, you can solve it quickly using a calculator. To divide using a calculator, enter the dividend first, then the division symbol, then the divisor and equal sign.

Solution: The correct answer is b.

TEST TIME: Show Your Work

Divide 5,412 ÷ 120. Write any
remainder as a fraction.

Follow the long division steps.

Solution:

$$
\begin{array}{r}
45\text{R}12 \\
120\,\overline{)\,5{,}412} \\
-480 \\
\hline
612 \\
-600 \\
\hline
12
\end{array}
$$

Write the remainder as a fraction.
Reduce the fraction to lowest terms.

$45\,^{12}/_{120} = 45\,^{1}/_{10}$

$5{,}412 \div 120 = 45\,^{1}/_{10}$

19. Division: Powers and Multiples of Ten

Divisor Powers of Ten

Divide 1,200 by 10 and 100.

Step 1: Use long division to divide 1,200 by 10.

$$
\begin{array}{r}
120 \\
10\,\overline{)\,1{,}200} \\
-10 \\
\hline
20 \\
-20 \\
\hline
00 \\
-0 \\
\hline
0
\end{array}
$$

$1{,}200 \div 10 = 120$

Step 2: Use long division to divide 1,200 by 100.

$$
\begin{array}{r}
12 \\
100\,\overline{)\,1{,}200} \\
-100 \\
\hline
200 \\
-200 \\
\hline
0
\end{array}
$$

$1{,}200 \div 100 = 12$

When you divide a number that ends in zeros by a power of ten, you can drop one zero off the end of the dividend for each zero in the divisor.

$1{,}200 \div 1\ \ = 1{,}200$

$1{,}200 \div 10\ = 120$

$1{,}200 \div 100 = 12$

When you can solve a problem mentally, do it and move quickly to the next problem. However, do not move so quickly that you misread the problem.

TEST TIME: Multiple Choice

6,000,000 ÷ 10,000 = _____

        a. 60
        ⓑ 600
        c. 6,000
        d. 60,000

10,000 is a power of 10 with 4 zeros. Drop 4 zeros from 6,000,000.

6,00̶0̶,0̶0̶0̶

Solution: The correct answer is b.

Multiples of Ten

Divide 6, 60, and 600 each by 2.

Step 1: Divide 6 by 2. This is a basic fact. $6 \div 2 = 3$

Step 2: Use long division to divide 60 by 2.

$$
\begin{array}{r}
30 \\
2\overline{)\ 60} \\
-6 \\
\hline
00 \\
-0 \\
\hline
0
\end{array}
$$

$60 \div 2 = 30$

Step 3: Use long division to divide 600 by 2.

$$
\begin{array}{r}
300 \\
2\overline{)\ 600} \\
-6 \\
\hline
00 \\
-0 \\
\hline
00 \\
-0 \\
\hline
0
\end{array}
$$

$600 \div 2 = 300$

When a dividend is a multiple of 10, you can take off the zeros to use a basic division fact. Put the same number of zeros back into the answer.

$6 \div 2 \quad = 3$
$60 \div 2 \quad = 30$
$600 \div 2 = 300$

TEST TIME: Multiple Choice

Jeremiah spent $1,600 on 80 boxes of nails.
What was the cost of each box?

> a. $2
> b. $16
> c. $20
> d. $40

This is a division problem: $1,600 ÷ 80. When both the dividend and divisor are multiples of ten, you can remove the same number of zeros from each without changing the answer.
$1,600 ÷ 80 = $160 ÷ 8.

Since 16 ÷ 8 = 2,

160 ÷ 8 = 20,

and 1,600 ÷ 80 = 20.

Solution: The correct answer is c.

Test-Taking Hint

Be careful to avoid careless answers on easy questions. Focus on each problem, and don't be in a hurry.

20. Dividing a Decimal

Decimals and Whole Numbers

Decimals are divided almost like whole numbers.

Divide 4.6 by 2.

Step 1: Write this problem using the long division symbol.

$$2 \overline{)4.6}$$

Step 2: Write the decimal point in the answer directly above the decimal point in the dividend.

$$2 \overline{)4.\overset{\bullet}{6}}$$

Step 3: Divide as you would a whole number.

$$
\begin{array}{r}
2.3 \\
2 \overline{)4.6} \\
\underline{-\ 4} \\
06 \\
\underline{-\ 6} \\
0
\end{array}
$$

4.6 ÷ 2 = 2.3

TEST TIME: Show Your Work

You have a choice of two packages of socks to buy. One has 3 pairs for $8.61. The other has 5 pairs for $13.15. Which is the better buy?

To find the better buy, you must find the cost of one pair of socks in each package. Divide each package cost by the number of pairs in that package. You can use a calculator to find the cost per pair or you can divide on paper and check your work with a calculator.

Solution: $8.61 ÷ 3 = $2.87
               $13.15 ÷ 5 = $2.63

The package with 5 pairs of socks costs less per pair, so it is the better buy.

Dividing Whole Numbers

Divide 1 ÷ 4.

Step 1: Write the problem using the long division symbol.

$$4\overline{)1}$$

Step 2: Write the number you are dividing as a decimal. Start with one zero. Place the decimal point in the answer.

$$4\overline{)1.0}$$

Step 3: Divide as you would a whole number. Add zeros and keep dividing until the remainder is zero.

$$
\begin{array}{r}
0.25 \\
4\overline{)1.00} \\
-8 \\
\hline
20 \\
-20 \\
\hline
0
\end{array}
$$

1 ÷ 4 = 0.25

TEST TIME: Multiple Choice

$2.7 \div 3 =$ ___

        a. 0.6

        (b.) 0.9

        c. 1.2

        d. 9

You can find this answer by knowing your basic facts and information about decimal multiplication. Ignore the decimal point. The basic fact is $27 \div 3 = 9$, which is the same as $3 \times 9 = 27$. Knowing about decimal multiplication tells you there are the same number of decimal places in the product as there are in the factors. There is one decimal place.

Solution: The correct answer is b.

Test-Taking Hint

Most tests are scored on the number of questions you answer correctly. You do not lose points for wrong answers. Answer every question, even if you have to guess.

21. Dividing by a Decimal

Decimals and Decimals

You can move the decimal point in a division problem, as long as you move it the same way in both numbers.

Divide 0.8 ÷ 1.6.

Step 1: Write the problem using the long division symbol.

$$1.6\,\overline{)0.8}$$

Step 2: Before you begin, make the divisor a whole number by moving the decimal point one place to the right. Move the decimal point in the dividend the same number of places.

$$16.\,\overline{)08.}$$

Step 3: Write the decimal point in the answer. Divide as you would a whole number.

$$
\begin{array}{r}
0.5 \\
16.\overline{)08.0} \\
-8\,0 \\
\hline
0
\end{array}
$$

0.8 ÷ 1.6 = 0.5

TEST TIME: Multiple Choice

There are 0.625 miles in one kilometer. How many kilometers are there in 17.5 miles?

> a. 10.9
> b. 27.5
> c. 28.0
> d. 28.5

To find the number of kilometers in 17.5 miles, you must divide by the number of miles in one kilometer.

Divide using either a calculator or a paper and pencil.

$17.5 \div 0.625 = 28.0$

Solution: The correct answer is c.

Test-Taking Hint

Read word problems carefully. Key words such as total, per, average, or difference can help you decide what operation should be performed.

Whole Numbers and Decimals

Divide 18 ÷ 0.4.

Step 1: Write the problem using the long division symbol.

$$0.4\overline{)18}$$

Step 2: Before you begin, make the divisor a whole number by moving the decimal point one place to the right. Move the decimal point in the dividend the same number of places. Remember, in a whole number like 18, the decimal point is at the end. Add zeros as needed to fill in the places on the right.

$$4\overline{)180}$$

Step 3: Now you have a whole number division problem. Divide.

$$
\begin{array}{r}
45 \\
4\overline{)180} \\
-16 \\
\hline
20 \\
-20 \\
\hline
0
\end{array}
$$

$18 \div 0.4 = 45$

TEST TIME: Show Your Work

A room has a floor area of 279 square feet.
The width of the room is 12.4 feet. What is the room's length?

The area of a room is found by multiplying length times width.
When the area and one of the dimensions are given, you can
find the missing dimension using division.

Solution: $279 \div 12.4$ $12.4\overline{)279}$ = $124\overline{)2790}$

$$
\begin{array}{r}
22.5 \\
124\overline{)2790} \\
-248 \\
\hline
310 \\
-248 \\
\hline
620 \\
-620 \\
\hline
0
\end{array}
$$

The room is 22.5 feet long.

Test-Taking Hint

Check your answers whenever you can. In the problem
above, you can check your answer using multiplication.
$22.5 \times 12.4 = 279$. Correct!

22. Dividing Fractions

Dividing a Fraction by a Fraction

To divide by a fraction, multiply by the reciprocal.

Divide 1/6 by 3/5.

Step 1: Write the problem using the division sign.

$$\frac{1}{6} \div \frac{3}{5}$$

Step 2: Rewrite the problem using a multiplication sign and the reciprocal.

$$\frac{1}{6} \times \frac{5}{3}$$

Step 3: Multiply.

$$\frac{1}{6} \times \frac{5}{3} = \frac{1 \times 5}{6 \times 3} = \frac{5}{18}$$

TEST TIME: Show Your Work

Joe had 20 feet of rope cut into pieces 5/6 foot long. How many pieces of rope did Joe have after it was cut?

The rope is divided into smaller pieces. This is a division problem.

Solution: 20 feet ÷ 5/6 foot pieces = number of pieces

20 ÷ 5/6

Write the whole number, 20, as an improper fraction.

$$\frac{20}{1} \div \frac{5}{6} = \frac{\overset{4}{\cancel{20}}}{1} \times \frac{6}{\underset{1}{\cancel{5}}} = \frac{4}{1} \times \frac{6}{1} = \frac{24}{1}$$

Joe had 24 pieces of rope.

Dividing by Unit Fractions

Shanya divided 7 quarts of chicken feed into 1/2-quart portions. How many portions did she have?

Step 1: You know the total, and you know the size of each smaller amount. This is a division problem.

$$7 \text{ quarts} \div \frac{1}{2} \text{ quart}$$

Step 2: Write the whole number as an improper fraction. Rewrite the problem using a multiplication sign and the reciprocal.

$$\frac{7}{1} \div \frac{1}{2} = \frac{7}{1} \times \frac{2}{1}$$

Step 3: Multiply.

$$\frac{7}{1} \times \frac{2}{1} = \frac{7 \times 2}{1 \times 1} = \frac{14}{1}$$

Shanya had 14 portions of feed.

Test-Taking Hint

Dividing by a unit fraction is easy. Just multiply by the denominator. For example, dividing by 1/2 is the same as multiplying by 2.

TEST TIME: Explain Your Answer

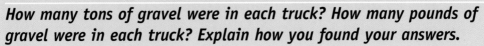

A gravel company divided 1/2 ton of gravel between 4 small trucks.

How many tons of gravel were in each truck? How many pounds of gravel were in each truck? Explain how you found your answers.

This problem asks for two measurement answers, one in tons, and one in pounds. It also asks for an explanation of how you found the answers. Be sure to include all of the required answers.

Solution: There is a total of 1/2 ton of gravel. To find the amount of gravel each truck gets in tons you must divide 1/2 ton by 4.

$$1/2 \div 4 = 1/2 \times 1/4 = 1/8$$

Each truck has 1/8 of a ton of gravel.

There are 2,000 pounds in a ton.

To find the amount of gravel each truck gets in pounds, multiply the number of pounds in a ton by the number of tons in a truck.

$$2{,}000 \times 1/8 = 2000/1 \times 1/8 = 250 \text{ pounds}$$

Each truck has 250 pounds of gravel.

23. Mixed Numbers

Renaming Mixed Fractions

Any mixed fraction can be renamed as an improper fraction.

Write $2\frac{3}{4}$ as an improper fraction.

Step 1: The numerator of the improper fraction is found by multiplying the whole number by the denominator, then adding the numerator from the mixed fraction.

$$(2 \times 4) + 3 = 11$$

Step 2: Write the improper fraction. The denominator is the same as the denominator in the fraction part of the mixed fraction.

$$\frac{11}{4}$$

Janice makes scarves to donate to a local shelter. She can make 6 scarves in one hour. If Janice works on making scarves for 5 $^{1}/_{3}$ hours, how many can she make?

a. 30

b. 32

c. 33

d. 35

To find the number of scarves Janice can make, multiply the number of hours she works by the number of scarves she can make per hour. Write the whole number and mixed fraction as improper fractions, then multiply.

$$6 \times 5\,^{1}/_{3} = \frac{\overset{2}{\cancel{6}}}{1} \times \frac{16}{\underset{1}{\cancel{3}}} = 32$$

Solution: Answer b is correct.

Divide Mixed Numbers

Divide 3 ³/₈ by 2 ¹/₄.

Step 1: Write each mixed fraction as an improper fraction.

$$3\frac{3}{8} \div 2\frac{1}{4} = \frac{27}{8} \div \frac{9}{4}$$

Step 2: Rewrite the problem using a multiplication sign and the reciprocal.

$$\frac{27}{8} \times \frac{4}{9}$$

Step 3: Simplify, then multiply.

$$\frac{3}{2} \times \frac{1}{1} = \frac{3 \times 1}{2 \times 1} = \frac{3}{2}$$

Step : Write the improper fraction as a mixed number.

$$\frac{3}{2} = 1\frac{1}{2}$$

Test-Taking Hint

You can go through a test and do the easy problems first. This can help you gain confidence, and keeps you from running out of time and missing easy points.

TEST TIME: Explain Your Answer

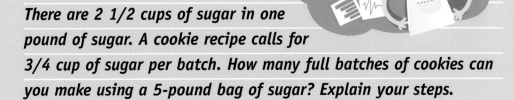

There are 2 1/2 cups of sugar in one pound of sugar. A cookie recipe calls for 3/4 cup of sugar per batch. How many full batches of cookies can you make using a 5-pound bag of sugar? Explain your steps.

Solution:

First, find the number of cups of sugar in a 5-pound bag.

Cups in 5-lb bag = pounds per bag × cups per pound

$$= 5 \times 2\frac{1}{2} = \frac{5}{1} \times \frac{5}{2} = \frac{25}{2}$$

$$= 12\frac{1}{2} \text{ cups per bag}$$

Then, find the number of batches you can make from $12\frac{1}{2}$ cups.

Number of batches = cups per bag ÷ cups per batch

$$= 12\frac{1}{2} \div \frac{3}{4} = \frac{25}{2} \div \frac{3}{4} = \frac{25}{2} \times \frac{4}{3} = \frac{50}{3}$$

$$= 16\frac{2}{3} \text{ batches}$$

You can make 16 full batches of cookies.

24. Estimation: Division

Compatible Numbers

One way to estimate using division is to use compatible numbers.

Estimate 55 ÷ 7.

Step 1: Compatible numbers are numbers that work well together. Look at the numbers in the problem. Let's think of this using multiplication.

55 ÷ 7 = __ can be written as 7 × __ = 55.

Step 2: Is there a basic multiplication fact for 7s that has a product close to 55?

$$7 \times 7 = 49$$
$$7 \times 8 = 56$$

Step 3: Estimate using the basic fact. Remember when you write your answer that it is an estimate. Use words such as *about* or *around*.

55 ÷ 7 is about 8.

Test-Taking Hint

Use estimation to check the results of exact answers.

TEST TIME: Show Your Work

Harrison spent $24.00 on 5 candles.
How much was each candle? Estimate to make sure your
answer is reasonable.

		$ 4.80
Solution:	$24.00 ÷ 5	5)$24.00
		− 20
		40
		− 40
		0

Harrison spent $4.80 on each candle.

$24.00 is close to $25.00.

25 ÷ 5 = 5.

$4.80 is close to $5.00. $4.80 is a reasonable answer.

TEST TIME: Show Your Work

Nettie scored 8.6, 5.2, 7.9, and 5.7 on her floor routine. About what was her average score?

To find an average, first add the scores, then divide by 4, which is the number of scores. You can estimate by rounding each score to the nearest whole number.

Solution: 8.6 + 5.2 + 7.9 + 5.7 is about
            9 + 5 + 8 + 6, or 28.

28 ÷ 4 = 7

Nettie's average score was around a 7.

Test-Taking Hint

Make sure you are answering the question that is asked. Some problems require more than one step. In the problem above, you can estimate the total of the scores, then divide to find an approximate average.

Powers and Multiples of Ten

Estimate the quotient of 44,264 ÷ 90.

Step 1: You can use powers and multiples of 10 along with compatible numbers to help estimate. Look at this as a multiplication problem.

44,264 ÷ 90 = ___ can be written as 90 × ___ = 44,264.

Step 2: The factor 90 is a multiple of 10. Look at the first few digits of the product. Is there a basic multiplication fact for 9s that has a product close to 44?

$$9 \times 4 = 36$$
$$9 \times 5 = 45$$

Step 3: Estimate using the basic fact and multiples of 10. Remember when you write your answer that it is an estimate. Use words such as *about* or *around*.

45 ÷ 9 is about 5, so
45,000 ÷ 90 is about 500.

44,264 ÷ 90 is about 500.

Further Reading

Books

Immergut, Britta, and Jean Burr Smith. *Arithmetic and Algebra Again: Leaving Math Anxiety Behind Forever*. New York: McGraw Hill, Inc., 2005.

McKellar, Danica. *Math Doesn't Suck: How to Survive Middle School Math Without Losing Your Mind or Breaking a Nail*. New York: Hudson Street Press, 2007.

Rozakis, Laurie. *Get Test Smart!: The Ultimate Guide to Middle School Standardized Tests*. New York: Scholastic Reference, 2007.

Internet Addresses

Coolmath.com. ***Coolmath's Long Division Lessons*** 1997–2010. <http://www.coolmath4kids.com/long-division/index.html>

MathIsFun.com, Inc. ***Learn Your Multiplication Tables.*** 2011. <http://www.mathisfun.com/tables.html>

Testtakingtips.com. ***Test Taking Tips.*** 2003–2010. <http://www.testtakingtips.com/test/math.htm>

Index

Index